D1298104

Girls Rock!

Fashion Design
Secrets

K. C. Kelley and John Willis

MEDIA ENHANCED BOOKS
AV2 BY WEIGL
ADDED VALUE · AUDIO VISUAL

www.av2books.com

AV² provides enriched content that supplements and complements this book. Weigl's AV² books strive to create inspired learning and engage young minds in a total learning experience.

Your AV² Media Enhanced books come alive with...

Audio
Listen to sections of the book read aloud.

Video
Watch informative video clips.

Embedded Weblinks
Gain additional information for research.

Try This!
Complete activities and hands-on experiments.

Key Words
Study vocabulary, and complete a matching word activity.

Quizzes
Test your knowledge.

Slide Show
View images and captions, and prepare a presentation.

... and much, much more!

Go to **www.av2books.com**, and enter this book's unique code.

BOOK CODE

H337347

AV² by Weigl brings you media enhanced books that support active learning.

Published by AV² by Weigl
350 5ᵗʰ Avenue, 59ᵗʰ Floor
New York, NY 10118
Website: www.av2books.com

Library of Congress Cataloging-in-Publication Data

Names: Kelley, K. C. and Willis, John.
Title: Fashion design secrets / K.C. Kelley and John Willis.
Description: New York, NY : AV2 by Weigl, [2017] | Series: Girls rock! |
   Reprint of: Mankato, Minn. : Child's World, 2009. -- (Reading rocks!). |
   Includes bibliographical references and index.
Identifiers: LCCN 2016004409 (print) | LCCN 2016004723 (ebook) | ISBN
   9781489647771 (hard cover : alk. paper) | ISBN 9781489650979 (soft cover :
   alk. paper) | ISBN 9781489647788 (Multi-user ebk.)
Subjects: LCSH: Fashion design--Vocational guidance--Juvenile literature |
   Fashion designers--Juvenile literature.
Classification: LCC TT507 .R675 2017 (print) | LCC TT507 (ebook) | DDC
   746.9/2--dc23
LC record available at http://lccn.loc.gov/2016004409

Printed in the United States of America in Brainerd, Minnesota
1 2 3 4 5 6 7 8 9 0   20 19 18 17 16

042016
041216

Project Coordinator: Katie Gillespie   Designer: Mandy Christiansen

Every reasonable effort has been made to trace ownership and to obtain permission to reprint copyright material. The publishers would be pleased to have any errors or omissions brought to their attention so that they may be corrected in subsequent printings.

Weigl acknowledges Getty Images, iStock, Corbis, and Shutterstock as its primary image suppliers for this title.

contents

1 Starting Out in Fashion

Take a moment to look around you. Everyone is wearing clothes, right? All those shirts, pants, dresses, skirts, sweatshirts, and even caps were designed by someone. Whether clothes are plain or fancy, for wearing everyday or for a special event, they're all part of fashion.

The business of fashion design started around 1858. That's when an Englishman named Charles Worth started a shop in Paris. He made clothes for the rich and famous. People visiting the store saw models wearing Worth's designs. If they liked the clothes, customers could then order copies made to fit themselves. Soon, other designers and shops followed Worth's way of making and selling clothes. By the early 1900s, Paris was the home of haute couture (OHT kuh-TYOOR), or "high fashion."

In his Paris store, Charles Worth created many beautiful gowns like this one.

Fashion companies today make millions of dollars designing and making clothes. People working at these companies work with colors, shapes, and styles. They choose from different fabrics and materials to make new clothing ideas. The creative people who come up with the ideas for new clothes are called fashion designers. They create the styles that people will wear. Designers also choose what fabrics are used and what colors will be popular.

There are three main areas of fashion design. Fashion designers usually specialize in one type of clothing. High fashion includes very expensive, one-of-a-kind outfits. These are sometimes made for just one person to wear— only once! Some high-fashion clothes are made just for movie or music stars.

Ready-to-wear clothes are less expensive than high-fashion ones. These styles are made for more people to buy. But these clothes are still made with very nice fabrics that are often too expensive for many people to buy.

Mass-market clothes are made in very large numbers and cost much less. Most of the clothes that everyday people wear are mass-market.

Celebrities such as Lady Gaga often show off the finest in high fashion.

With all the types of clothing in the world, fashion companies must be organized. Most companies focus on just one type of clothing. Larger companies, however, might make clothes for lots of different people. These companies hire designers who can create many different styles.

Fashion designers work with other people in a company to determine the types of clothes people are likely to buy in the coming year. They must work many months ahead of when the clothes will actually be sold. That's because designing and making clothes takes a long time. For instance, a designer might work all winter on clothes that won't be sold until summertime!

Types of Clothing

Most designers and companies work in one main area of fashion. These are the most popular areas of the fashion world:

- Women's wear
- Teens
- Sportswear
- Underwear
- Bridal wear

- Menswear
- Children's
- Outerwear
- Evening wear*
- Accessories**

Fancy clothes such as tuxedos or ball gowns.
**Extra items to wear or use, such as purses, hats, scarves, or bags.*

Most fashion designers learn how to do their jobs at fashion schools. They study art, design, fabrics, sewing, and other areas. A fashion designer must have a great sense of style and understand how color and line work on a person's body. They have to be very good at drawing, too.

At school, young designers draw ideas for new styles. They might change a drawing many times before they're happy with it. When ready, a designer will actually cut fabrics and sew together the pieces for their new design.

Student designers cut fabrics for their ideas after carefully measuring each piece.

At the end of their schooling, designers have a portfolio of their work. This shows companies the kinds of clothes the designer is good at creating.

Most designers start out as assistants. They might work for a large company or for a small studio.

Sew What?

Even the most famous fashion designers began their careers sewing. If you want to create clothing, you should know how to sew. Once you learn to use a sewing machine, you can make almost anything— from a pillowcase to a formal gown!

2 Here Comes the Fashion!

How do fashion designers create their masterpieces? It takes a lot of imagination, planning, skill, and hard work. First, designers watch the world around them. They look at the colors, shapes, and fabrics that people are wearing—and then they try to guess what those same people will want to wear in the future. Designers look at fashion magazines to see which styles are popular. They visit stores to see other designers' ideas. And they always keep their eyes out for new kinds of fabrics.

Since fashion changes with every season, most companies put out new styles twice a year—in the spring and in the fall. But just when one season's collection has been designed, sewn, and shipped to stores, it's time to start designing the next season's clothes!

Fashion magazines feature beautiful models wearing all the latest styles.

A designer's **collection** includes all the clothes that he or she has **designed** for that season.

Fashion designers use pencils, pens, and colored markers to create sketches of new clothing.

Let's follow along as fashion designers turn their ideas into clothes for you to wear. First, designers sketch their ideas onto large paper pads. They try different shapes, lengths, and cuts. They might play around with colors or add details like buttons or flaps. This is the fun part for most designers—when their imaginations can run wild!

Designers must always keep their customers in mind. If a design is too silly or uncomfortable, people won't want to buy it. Designers work with lots of fabrics to decide which ones work best with their ideas. They drape the fabrics on dummies. This helps designers see how different fabrics lay on a person's body. Out of all this thinking, drawing, and draping comes ideas for some great new clothes.

Fashion **dummies** are used to show how clothing will fit on people.

The next step is to make a sample of the design. Some designers create samples themselves, but many work with seamstresses. First, fabric is cut to the right size and shape. Then the pieces are loosely sewn together. Sewing the sample loosely lets the designer make adjustments. This early-stage piece is sometimes called a muslin after the inexpensive fabric it's made with.

The muslin is loosely draped and stitched on the dummy to see how the new design fits.

The designer will work with the muslin to make the piece look just right. She might make the dress longer or change the shape of the sleeve or neck. She might take it apart and put it back together many times before it's finally done.

Then it's time to use the real fabric to make a full sample. The designer also chooses buttons, ribbons, and other pieces of trim.

After choosing the fabric, the designer sews some pieces together to make a sample.

Often a designer will put the handmade sample on a real-life model. Seeing how a person moves in the piece shows the designer a lot. Does the dress move well around the model's legs? Can her arms move well in the sleeves? Is the neck too high or too low? From the original idea, many changes have been made.

Designers measure and check each part to make sure everything fits together correctly.

Once the designer is happy with the sample, another worker makes a **pattern** out of paper. This is a bit like a jigsaw puzzle of all the parts. This pattern will be used to make sure that every copy of the piece of clothing is the same.

Some **sewing** stores sell **patterns** that you can use to make your own **clothes**.

There are hundreds of different fabrics—and colors— for designers to choose from!

The paper pattern is used to cut the fabric into the right shapes. Then the pieces are sewn together, either with large machines (for mass-market clothes) or by hand (for haute couture outfits). Large factories can turn out hundreds or thousands of pieces in just hours.

Large factories like this one can create lots of copies of a piece of clothing in a short time.

It has taken many hours of hard work, and lots of new ideas and changes, but the fashion designer has done it. She has taken her new idea from some pencil sketches and turned them into clothing for people to wear.

But the work of the fashion designer is far from over!

Ecofashion

Like many people, fashion designers today are concerned with the **environment**. Some designers are starting to use materials that are recycled or that don't harm the environment. Designer Lara Miller, for example, makes clothes from the scraps of old T-shirts. She also makes clothes from bamboo, a type of grass that grows quickly.

3 The show and the Store

All that hard work is just a part of the designer's job. She and other designers will make many new pieces for their fashion company. Together, these new clothes make up a "line."

How do designers choose which clothes to include in their company's lines? First, they talk to the owners of the stores in which the clothes will be sold.

These people know their customers. They know the types of clothes that their customers will buy. Designers also try to follow **trends**, which are a little like fads. For example, perhaps bright colors are the trend for spring, while denim clothing is popular in the fall.

A store will often display the pieces of a company's line all together.

Most companies tell people about their new lines by holding fashion shows. These can be very glamorous events. The most important fashion shows are held in New York City, London, and Paris. Hundreds of people from the fashion world come together to watch models show off the new clothes. Dressed in all types of clothes, the models walk down a runway. Sometimes they pose or twirl. Fashion fans fill the seats along the sides of the runway. Bright lights and loud music make the shows fun and exciting.

Just Showing Off

Most fashion shows feature clothes that people might see in stores. But some shows feature clothes that are just wonderful creations designers want to show off. These pieces might be one-of-a-kind dresses or amazing outfits. There might be strange fabrics or wild shapes. These are not clothes that you'll see in stores, but when these artful pieces hit the runway, fashion fans take notice!

After being featured in fashion shows, clothes are often advertised in magazines. They soon arrive in stores, where customers try them on ... and hopefully buy them! As pieces begin to sell, the designer is still working. She studies information from the stores to see which clothes are selling well. Sometimes a magazine or Web site will write a review of the new clothes. Do people like them? Do they dislike them? The designer wants to know! All this information will help her shape the next line of clothes.

People working in clothing stores make sure that the designers' work is ready for customers.

Soon it's back to the drawing pad for the fashion designer. She and other people at her company must begin coming up with new designs for the season ahead.

After the clothes are in the stores, it's back to the drawing pad for designers!

The world of fashion is an exciting, creative, and busy place. If you love clothes and fashion, there are many ways in which you can join this world. Becoming a fashion designer is one way, of course. Practice your drawing skills by creating dresses, pants, shirts ... or whatever.

Ask your parents to help you get some fabrics, and start experimenting with different ideas. It would also be good to learn how to sew. Knowing how clothes are put together can give you new ideas for designs.

Fashion design makes up half of all home sewing projects in the United States.

Reading about clothing and fashion can also be helpful. Your knowledge of fashion might help you sell clothes to stores. And as you get older, you might even work at a clothing store to learn more about what customers like to buy.

What's the best way to enter the world of fashion? Just open your closet and start having fun with your own clothes!

Quiz

1 What is the first step when making a new clothing design?

A: Sketching ideas on a pad

2 What type of clothes do most people wear?

A: Mass-market

3 What plant does Lara Miller use to make clothes?

A: Bamboo

4 How often do companies usually put out new styles?

A: Twice a year

5 What area of design makes one-of-a-kind pieces?

A: High fashion

6 How do most companies tell people about their new lines?

A: With fashion shows

7 When did the business of fashion design begin?

A: 1858

8 What area of fashion includes ball gowns and tuxedos?

A: Evening wear

9 Where do most fashion designers learn how to do their job?

A: At fashion schools

10 What do designers use fashion magazines for?

A: To see what styles are popular

Key Words

collection a group of clothes put out by a fashion company

designed created new types of clothing ideas by sketching and sewing

drape laying cloth on a dummy or a person to see how a piece of clothing might look

dummies soft, headless statues used to model and fit clothing

environment the land, air, plants, and water all around us

glamorous very fancy

haute couture French words meaning "high fashion"

line how clothing fits on a person's body; also, a group of clothes put out by a fashion company

muslin an early version of a sample

pattern the paper outline used to show the shape or shapes that will make up a piece of clothing

portfolio a collection of drawings by a fashion designer

review an article that gives someone's opinion about an event or a line of clothing

runway the long walkway used in fashion shows

sample the first version of a piece, before it has been perfected and sold to customers

seamstresses people who sew

specialize to focus on just one type of thing (in this case, one type of clothing)

studio a small design company or a small group of designers

trends fads that show the kind of clothing most people are wearing

Index

Log on to www.av2books.com

AV² by Weigl brings you media enhanced books that support active learning. Go to www.av2books.com, and enter the special code found on page 2 of this book. You will gain access to enriched and enhanced content that supplements and complements this book. Content includes video, audio, weblinks, quizzes, a slide show, and activities.

AV² Online Navigation

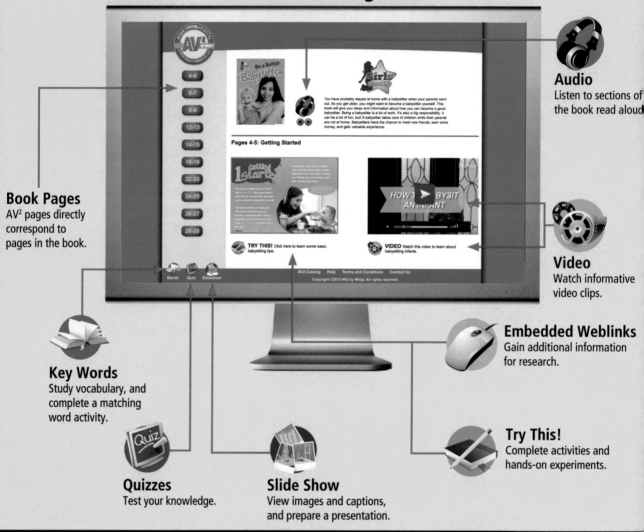

Audio
Listen to sections of the book read aloud

Video
Watch informative video clips.

Embedded Weblinks
Gain additional information for research.

Try This!
Complete activities and hands-on experiments.

Book Pages
AV² pages directly correspond to pages in the book.

Key Words
Study vocabulary, and complete a matching word activity.

Quizzes
Test your knowledge.

Slide Show
View images and captions, and prepare a presentation.

AV² was built to bridge the gap between print and digital. We encourage you to tell us what you like and what you want to see in the future.

Sign up to be an AV² Ambassador at www.av2books.com/ambassador.

Due to the dynamic nature of the Internet, some of the URLs and activities provided as part of AV² by Weigl may have changed or ceased to exist. AV² by Weigl accepts no responsibility for any such changes. All media enhanced books are regularly monitored to update addresses and sites in a timely manner. Contact AV² by Weigl at 1-866-649-3445 or av2books@weigl.com with any questions, comments, or feedback.